MW01595443

# POSITIONING YOURSELF

FOR

# MONEY MIRACLES

BRENDA KUNNEMAN

One Voice Ministries
P.O. Box 390460
Omaha, NE 68139
855-777-7907
www.hankandbrenda.org


Positioning Yourself for Money Miracles
ISBN 978-0-9970645-2-0

# TABLE OF CONTENTS

# CHAPTER ONE
## The God of Money Miracles

At some point in life everyone has experienced a financial need, even very serious ones at times. Often such needs can require a practical financial solution to pay an unexpected or costly debt or bill. At times it may have required a sudden dramatic turnaround, or even a total miracle.

In fact, the need for ongoing material provision affects every human life on this planet. Of course we all need provision and finances to buy food, clothing, and to sustain the most basic needs of life. In addition to that, financial supply also adds to a certain level of fulfillment in human lives. Obviously everyone feels some measure of happiness when they either get something new or simply own nice things. What is to be avoided is covetousness that excludes God and replaces Him with a love of money and things. Without God, even the best material things are empty and lifeless.

Unfortunately, the challenges that surround this present life can put pressure on our monetary supply and sustenance of life. We live in a world that suffers from the curse of Adam's fall; therefore the financial toil of life is part of our daily struggle. Because of that, there are times our finances can feel low to the point of discouragement or even becoming terrifying.

The Apostle Paul communicated this struggle of life so plainly when he said, *"I know both how to be abased, and I know how to abound: everywhere and in all things I am instructed both to be full and to be hungry, both to abound and to suffer need."* (see Philippians 4:12) Paul wasn't saying this because it's God's desire that we suffer painfully regarding material provision. He was saying that he learned how to trust God when life presents financial pressure and how to walk through it into victory.

How do we know that is true? We know because in verse 19 of the same chapter Paul also exclaims with confidence and faith, *"But my God shall supply all your need according to his riches in glory by Christ Jesus."* If you were to paraphrase his words, you might say *"Even when the supply seems a little low, I know how to remain steady through it because in the end my God will supply!"* He learned the confidence to say that in every situation he could trust God to be the source that would meet his need.

I once heard a person say that financial pressure is one of the worst kinds of pressure one can ever face. That is true to a great extent. Financial pressure can affect one's health, place stress on marriages and relationships, and it can cause immobilizing fear.  It's a source of lost sleep for countless people who are staring at a mounting pile of bills, calls from creditors, or perhaps can't pay their mortgage or rent and don't know where their next meal is coming from.

In Scripture, Paul communicated how he learned to face this roller coaster of such pressures through God's grace knowing that God would supply for every need in some way, somehow, and in some miraculous fashion.  I would assume he built that confidence not only from personal experience, but also by personally knowing that God truly cares about these basic areas of our lives.  In fact, God cares about these areas so much that He will even at times perform financial miracles to ensure our well-being.

Just given the impressive affect financial pressure can place on a person's wellbeing, it stands to reason that God, who loves us without measure, wants to be involved in all aspects of our financial concerns.  Truthfully, one of the predominant messages of Scripture is God's message of miraculous financial supply.

We see it with Adam and Eve when God gave them every good thing they could possibly want or need in the garden.  We saw it with Noah in the Ark, as it could only have been supernatural how God supplied (or perhaps made certain Noah knew how to supply) for all the animals in addition to his family on board the boat for such a long time.  One can only call that a "money miracle" of tremendous proportions!

Then, of course we know of Abraham and how God

introduced Himself as Abraham's salary and source of supply (Genesis 15:1).  From there we go to Isaac and Jacob who prospered in all they did.  Joseph became ruler of Egypt, whom God anointed to feed a nation in a time of famine.  On it goes to Moses and the children of Israel, in their escape from slavery and through the wilderness God gave them what we would refer to today as nothing less than "money miracles." Their supply was supernaturally provided for and it was because God was with them.

The prophets of the Old Testament also experienced God's money miracles.  We see it with Elijah who was fed of ravens and Elisha who brought a fallen axe head back to the surface of the water saving the financial situation of a man in need. We saw it with David in whom God granted the entire nation of Israel, and with Solomon the wealthiest king in biblical history.

These are only a few examples of money miracles, but the examples continue into the New Testament where we read of Jesus whom history indicates was supplied for in life not only through His parents, but by the magi.  Those magi offered Jesus gifts that were of exceptional monetary value. His ministry was also supported by the wealth of many who followed Him including the wife of Chuza, Herod's business manager, who was known to have been wealthy (see Luke 8:3).

Jesus further exemplified money miracles from heaven when He supernaturally fed 5,000 men and a multitude of women and children.  At one point the disciples asked Jesus if He wanted them to go purchase food for the crowd (see Mark 6:36-37).  We can only assume they either had the money already or expected a money miracle to occur so they could do so!

With all that said, each of these who received money miracles also had to position themselves to receive them.  They had to walk with God, agree with Him and follow His patterns and principles.  Without doing so, they would have gone in the wrong direction back toward the curse and the hard pathway that this life so often presents.

God has a pattern so you can experience money miracles too.  He does not want you to struggle through life in a destitute way.  He is the God who has promised provision.  Jesus preached this very sermon in Matthew Chapter 6.  In verse 31 He says, *"Therefore take no thought, saying, What shall we eat? Or, What shall we drink? Or, Wherewithal shall we be clothed?"*  He was reminding us that we must learn to let these financial worries fall into God's hands who knows we have need of these things (see Matthew 6:32).  Jesus finishes His profound speech on monetary provision by saying, *"But seek ye first the kingdom of God, and his righteousness; and all these things shall be added unto you."* (Matthew 6:33)

What He was communicating, in a nutshell, was that God is truly interested in your financial situation enough to perform a miracle when needed.  Even beyond that, in the Bible we see that to an extent God also cares about our material wants and desires.  Jesus then reminds us, in Matthew 6:33, as part of the same sermon, that our life can't be wrapped up in fret over money.  Instead, we need to transfer any tendency toward financial fear to the Lord, who will see to it that we are taken care of.

God is so committed to your financial and material stability that He is committed to supply a miracle when it's needed, just as He did for the people of the Bible.  They were real people with real needs just like you and me.

What you must know today is that you serve a God who does do money miracles and will do them on your behalf if you get in agreement and alignment with Him.  No, God isn't all about just spoiling us with pointless indulgences, but He does want us blessed and fulfilled in this present life.  Included in that can be our personal desires, especially when we are sold out to God and His purposes.  I have seen God not only meet my personal needs, but grant many desires in my lifetime in very supernatural and miraculous ways.  Many of those desires had little or nothing to do with anything eternal, such as the need for new carpet or furnishings that I really liked!

My point is that I have been the recipient of money miracles from God, both in the ministry and in my own life.  I am not special beyond any of God's people, but I am committed to God's principles and His work.  God is the God who will supply money miracles for His people.  We just need to position ourselves to receive them!

# CHAPTER TWO
## The Miracle of Expectation

One of the key reasons why people don't receive money miracles is because they simply don't expect them. While that sounds so simple, it's actually fairly complicated!

We human beings, who are daily faced with our fallible sin nature, have a tremendous tendency to emphasize and focus upon the negative circumstances of life instead of the positive ones. Sure, some people have a stronger positive outlook than others, but the truth is that negative expectation is an ongoing battle that everyone must be aware of and overcome.

Think about it, you can have countless people who spoke kindly to you all day long, but it's that one person with a nasty attitude that mistreated you in some way that you went and told everyone about. You can have many faithful friends, but it's that one betrayer that seems to fill your mind. It's the eccentric and outlandish person in the mall and not the poised sales clerk that gets mentioned.  It's the insane driver that is screamed about, not all the hundreds of people who didn't attempt to run us off the road that day.  It's the family vacation gone awry that you tell your grandkids about, not so much the picture perfect memories; and on and on the scenarios go, it's comical but true.

Experiences are most often the unsaid culprit to our negative expectations which therefore become our consumed focus.  A person who has fought through a terrible or acute illness will commonly have some concern about or even fear a relapse.  For example, those who have had a heart attack will often fear a second, so much that they immediately enact dramatic lifestyle changes that they ignored prior to the attack, even when their doctor had encouraged them to do so previously.

Consider how after a terrible accident or injury many people often fear the thing surrounding the accident, such as riding in a car or walking on icy sidewalks in the winter time.  Think of how those who have been in abusive relationships so often struggle developing healthy relationships because their past pain is often a reference point that affects their present approach to people.

Negative experiences can teach us caution for the future, but they can also impress within our soul a tendency toward a negative expectation.   Of course, we who understand not only human nature but also the spirit realm know that demonic entities capitalize on this tendency of ours.  They will press heavily upon those experiences in their attempt to not only create negative expectation, but also create fears, anxiety, and a host of other evil strongholds.

Let me talk more about this reality for a moment. When I was a child, my dad was in the military and during an active duty tour we were stationed in the Pacific in a very tropical, humid climate. I was in grade school then and loved playing outside, daily if possible! I would spend hours riding my bike all over the military base with my friends, so much that I wouldn't stop to come in unless mom called, or it was absolutely necessary. That meant if I encountered minor scrapes and bumps that kids often get while playing, I wouldn't go home unless I was pretty much profusely bleeding. I was intensely active so such minor scrapes weren't uncommon, but I ignored those little cuts whenever possible.

However, in those dense, tropical climates, bugs and flies are extremely abundant. I can remember having mild wounds here and there and if I would stand still just long enough, multiple flies would begin to try and congregate on any open wound they could find. Sounds disgusting I know, but my point is that this is exactly how demons operate.
Demons look at our negative experiences and see them as an open wound of the soul. They already know how negative experiences affect the average person. They know that these experiences will often result in heightened caution and apprehension. So using that, like a fly or maggot, they "land upon" those emotions and memories like flies on a bleeding sore.

Depending on the severity of the negative, they will take already damaged emotions and literally attempt to abuse you with them in effort to drive you into bondages and fears on many levels. However, at minimum, if demons can't bind a person with serious fears and phobias, they will do all they can to at least get that person to fear that the same negative could reoccur. Then, if possible, the same demons will attempt to get that person to question the reliability of God's protection and provision.

I am sure you can relate to what I am saying here. So how does that affect our expectation concerning finances? Well, think of the financial challenges of your life and how they have affected you.

It's common knowledge that the way most people grow up, from an economic standpoint, is quite often how they end up. While that isn't true in every case (some kids have been far more successful than their parents or ancestors), it is still a common pattern. I hear people so many times say, "I am the first person in my family to graduate high school or college." Others, after finally buying their first home or new car often say, "No person in my family ever bought a house or new car." Perhaps you have said similar things regarding some scenario in your life and family history.

What these people are saying is they were the first who broke the cycle from a group where the individuals kept following the same negative patterns. While I am no psychologist, I am in the people business and I see again and again how people follow such patterns, often unknowingly. If something negative is a part of the pattern they experienced day by day, year after year, that is most commonly the pattern they follow without realizing it.

Add that to one's own personal negative experiences and people will, more often than not, walk through life indirectly believing that this is the road God intended for them. It becomes their expectation. No matter how many times you tell them God has a better plan for them, that He doesn't want them broke, or that He will provide for them in a supernatural way, they will still expect the same old negatives they have known all their life. They will even adapt their entire life habits, attitudes, and conversations accordingly.

Negative expectation is a tool of the devil! It's a tool to get your expectation off of the Lord and onto the pressures of life that our natural eyes continually see.

If we fall into that trap, we will never break the horrible pattern of failure. If the cycle doesn't get broken, we not only expect negative things, we speak negative things and therefore live out the same negative things repeatedly.

The greatest reformers of the Bible weren't perfect. In fact, you will find that many of them had negative expectations too. But if you study their lives, typically there came a moment that they had to stare negative expectation in the eye and decide that if God was for them nothing could be against them.

Sure, maybe your parents were poor and got a bad set up in life. Maybe your negative expectation comes from that experience or maybe it's from your age, ethnicity, gender, education, or current financial status. It's hard to break free from those visions in your mind, especially when a myriad of personal and painful emotions are involved regarding you or perhaps family members.

Countless people throughout history defied the odds with their own shift toward positive expectation. So imagine what happens if we not only utilize that element, but then take it to another level and get God involved! When God is involved the negatives can shift into divine positives at any moment. God is not limited to the dismal limitation of our mental negatives. If you continue to expect lack, poverty, joblessness, debt and shortages (for whatever reason they've occurred), or because that's what experience tells you to expect, then that is what you will live out. Don't limit God to that!

What could happen if you decide that the level you are living at needs to change? What if today you begin to determine that your level of education, that is perhaps limited to a certain salary level, needs to improve? What if you decide it's time to become skilled at something new and more financially gainful? Ask yourself, what is your expectation today?

Think of what happens when we not only change our internal and emotional periscope, but what happens when our expectation begins to involve a miraculous God. Not only can the right natural expectation change our perception on life, but once you add the God of miracles to the equation, anything incredible can happen!

Changing your expectation begins with a daily choice until it becomes a habit. Treat each day uniquely and see yourself succeeding. Do the things that will make any person successful. The list can be lengthy here, but most of us know that getting up daily and putting our hands to productive tasks will begin to cultivate success, whether those tasks are spiritual, social, occupational, or emotional. The shift doesn't happen overnight, but it does continually change with each positive choice we make.

Secondly, when challenges arise, don't repeatedly complain and give voice to them. Oh, how easy it is to talk about our negatives and bad days! It's even easier now with social media available where we can soapbox our lives and get others to comment and coddle to our current afflictions.

Change your voice to one of expectation instead. From there, begin to look to the God who intervenes in the most unexpected ways. I certainly will not pretend to know why people go through some of the difficult or even tragic things they do and wonder why God didn't prevent it. I do, however, believe that negative expectation in multiple areas can certainly contribute to such things on so many levels. Negative expectation can wear many masks such as condemnation, rejection, excessive confidence, or even depression.

While I can't speak to every unique circumstance along those lines, I do know that having a determined and regular expectation in a faithful and supernatural God, who is committed to your well-being, is the cultivating ground for miracles.   Just like the "flies" or demonic spirits from the enemy are attracted to the negative energy we emit, the Spirit of God is attracted to our confident faith that emits positive expectation.

God is attracted to your expectation expressing that He will provide in all circumstances of life, even when those circumstances might look a little bleak at times.  His attraction to intervene in your situation may manifest in many ways you wouldn't normally think of, but when you expect a divine intervention instead of always rehearsing what didn't happen or work out right, God is attracted to that.

Expect and envision God seeing you through your present financial storm.  Actually, if God wasn't already seeing you through, you wouldn't be reading this book right now!  But the fact is, you're still here, you're alive and if you can believe it, despite whatever happened yesterday, last week, or last year, then a miracle is on the way with your name on it.

Seriously ask yourself what you are expecting today.  Is the God of money miracles being attracted to your positive expectation?  If you are expecting that suddenly something will change for the better with your finances or that you will see yourself better off this time next year, then your miracle has already begun.  Miracles from God are seeded by our expectations, so let the miracle of positive expectation begin to work within you today!

# CHAPTER THREE
## The Harvest Factor

Everyone knows that you cannot have a harvest without seed. You can't expect crops without planting, and it's impossible to get results without effort or some form of investment. You don't look forward to the weekend without first enduring the workweek! It's a fact of life, but in the mind of many believers it's becoming a less than embraced truth when it comes to spiritual things.

This is likely due in part because in today's world, much more than the world of our parents and grandparents, people want something for nothing and lots of payoff with little effort. We label it today as the entitlement culture, those who want benefits without the blood, sweat, and tears that create those benefits.

The funny thing is that God is the one who invented the work toward payday cycle of life.  Jesus said, *"Give, and it shall be given unto you; good measure, pressed down, and shaken together, and running over, shall men give into your bosom. For with the same measure that ye mete withal it shall be measured to you again."* (Luke 6:38)  This saying from Jesus isn't only a church offering verse, which is how it's most commonly used, but instead is a principle for daily living.

Jesus was saying that if you invest in anything there is eventually a payout in some form, somewhere, at some point in the future.  He clarified that with the effort you put into something, whether it be little or much, that is the measure of results you will receive.  For example, you can't pour water endlessly into a glass without eventually experiencing overflow.  But if you pour just a little, there will be just a little water in the glass.

The Apostle Paul further emphasized this truth in Galatians 6:7 saying, *"Be not deceived; God is not mocked: for whatsoever a man soweth, that shall he also reap."*  In other words, don't deceive yourself with the notion that things can operate a different way and that you can enjoy results without effort.  On the flip side, don't believe you can do things you shouldn't and not expect negative consequences.

Think of this, if you eat fast food day and night there is a result, albeit a bad one, but a result nonetheless.  Now on the contrary, if you eat right and exercise daily there is another result, a positive one this time, but a result just the same.  If you study hard in school, there are beneficial results to it, but if you ignore homework and class assignments, once again... results. If you clean your home and pick up after yourself regularly the payoff is a clean and enjoyable atmosphere in which to live. If you work hard and pay your bills there are benefits to this consistency.

Everything in life is investment and payoff oriented. This fact can't be avoided under any circumstances. We can't be jealous of people living in certain blessings if we aren't willing to put forth the same effort and pay the same prices of hard effort they perhaps did on many levels. The cycle of "you get what you give" will always continue without fail and will be the life-long toil of every person alive, Christian or not. Give and it shall be given. It's how the earth functions.

So it's very obvious that there is nothing in this life that isn't based on the investment principle, yet somehow when it comes to God, we want His benefits, but often with far less investment than we might put into other things. However, if we want the God of money miracles regularly involved and watching over our financial lives then we must have the same unwavering dedication to invest finances into His Kingdom. Remember, no seed equals no harvest, and little seed results in a little harvest, abundant seed results in abundant harvest, and so on. And I believe you could also say that inconsistent or intermittent seed investment results in inconsistent and intermittent harvesting as well.

Receiving money miracles from God calls us to examine our investment level into the Kingdom of God because the seed time and harvest factor cannot be ignored.  It's working in our lives whether we want it to our not.

If our financial investment of giving into God and His work is negligent we shouldn't expect our financial lives to be safely under the covering of God's supernatural blessing.  That isn't because God doesn't love us and doesn't want to supply these blessings, it's because we aren't giving Him sufficient investment to work with and the results become limited.

As a pastor, over the years I've heard some people complain about investing their money into God's Kingdom.  They complain about tithing and want it to be an outdated truth. They feel like preachers are just trying to manipulate them out of their money when they ask for regular offerings for projects and programs.  Some feel like preachers talk about money too much, and on and on the reasons go.  Of course not everyone responds this way, but it's a reoccurring attitude that has surrounded the church world for years.  It even existed in Paul's day, as he reminded the Corinthian church that they shouldn't give grudgingly, but cheerfully and willingly (see 2 Corinthians 9:7).

What is unfortunate is that people will invest in all sorts of temporal things such as products, memberships, programs, or material goods and never once question if they are being manipulated, even though many of these secular companies hire marketing professionals whose entire goal is to manipulate you into responding!  That is why the fast food chains tantalize your eyes with a juicy burger on the television screen.  Have you ever stopped by the burger joint after seeing a commercial like that?  The answer is probably yes, but if not for that, at some time it was yes to something!

So when good pastors or ministries ask for support, so they can expand the Kingdom of God on multiple levels, we shouldn't shy away from it.  Instead, see it as an amazing opportunity to invest in something eternal that is connected to a God who has promised to supply financial breakthrough for those who do so.  To me it sounds like the best opportunity around and it's not limited to this mortal, temporary life on earth like other things are.  It's an eternal investment that changes lives and helps people find and experience Jesus.  It's not surprising that the enemy fights church giving so vehemently.

We should feel even more confident when we invest in ministries who have not only proven responsible fruit, but that are building up our lives personally.  If you are being uplifted, fed, and are growing spiritually from your local church then you should be committed to sow your finances abundantly into it.  Why wouldn't you want to give back for what you have received there?

The point is that you simply cannot have the blessing without considering the seed and harvest factor.  Sure God may bless us at times despite our negligent actions, but that isn't how we can always expect things to be.  The seed time and harvest factor, when it comes to financial miracles, is something God expects His children to grow in as we mature in our walk with

Him. It's going to work regardless, so we might as well get on the right side of things regarding it.

When I've heard people argue over the doctrine of tithing 10% into their church, I always think, "Why wouldn't you want to put 10% into God's work through your church? Isn't God's work and the church that you enjoy each week worth that much to you?" For myself, I have never struggled with the concept of tithing, and I want Jesus to have at least 10% of what I earn. I want Him to be my highest financial priority. Above my tithe I want to give Him offerings because more than anything else I want the Kingdom of God to be established in this world and it can't happen without the resources to do so.

God doesn't want His children to make tithing and giving offerings a point of doctrinal debate. He wants it to be a heart issue and something you don't have to do, but want to do. And honestly, from a perspective of principle, it just isn't right to expect God to supply financial breakthrough and miracles or watch over our finances when we are half-hearted or resistant about our financial giving into His work. It's sad that some people will ask for prayer, seek God for financial help, and so on, but never address their lack of tithing and giving. It truly isn't right to expect God to be there for us when we aren't committed in these areas. Now He may bail us out of a jam, but that doesn't make it right for us to treat God like Santa Clause, always giving our list of needs but not giving our resources back to Him.

This isn't meant to sound harsh, it's meant to help. We all need God covering our finances with His blessing, but to have it we can't ignore the issue of investment into the Kingdom, because the seed and harvest factor of life is working regardless. And in an earthly time when national economies are being severely challenged, we certainly need God's principles working on our behalf more than ever.

On the other hand, if you are sitting here reading this and thinking, "Lord, I hear this message loud and clear, but my finances are such a mess that I don't have two dimes to even give right now!" Maybe you are already so behind on bills that you are paying out everything you have to just keep the creditors off your back. It's not that your heart isn't for God, but you are just trying to stay afloat. Know today that God is not uncompassionate to understand your situation and He will work with you, but He looks for effort on your part to make changes.

Here is my common answer to that problem. Start somewhere and absolutely stay consistent. Period. Stay with something, whatever that is no matter what. Then as each month passes, increase your giving to God. Increase a little every month. Make a goal that by this time next year, as certain bills get paid down and so forth, that you won't rack up unnecessary new bills, but that God will now become a priority in your plans and budgeting.

When it comes to tithing, start somewhere and make a determined effort that you will ultimately tithe 10%. When your pastor receives a special offering (which should be separate from your tithe) for an event, project, or program, don't let the opportunity pass by you. Every time you invest in God's work, God is noting it and getting involved in your financial life. You are setting yourself up to receive a harvest of blessing and to receive money miracles!

No, it may not all happen in one day, and this doesn't mean challenges won't arise that have to be worked out over time. What it means is that when challenges do come, you will have faith and confidence that your investment with God is working for you. At the same time, when you put God's investment principles into place, there will also be financial miracles that will bring sudden divine turnarounds!

God can bring miracles in many ways we don't expect and we don't have to worry ourselves figuring that part out. What you can be sure of is that when you have that investment in place, He is working on your financial behalf someplace, somewhere, and somehow. A lost job may just mean a better job. A lost business may just mean less pressure and a new occupation in which you are much happier. Something broken may just mean a replacement you didn't have to pay for. You never know with God, anything good can happen! Our job is to put the investment in place and let Him do the rest! God's seed time and harvest factor will always set us up for the miraculous, if we embrace it!

# CHAPTER FOUR
## Breaking Financial Strongholds

Seeing turnaround in our financial lives involves many elements. It's certainly not an overnight process and is not typically an easy one. It involves daily choices such as keeping a careful budget, watching one's spending, and so forth. It behooves each person to learn basic money management skills, particularly if they weren't taught growing up. Being financially responsible works for everyone, whether Christian or not. At the same time, I want to spend some time discussing how the spirit realm affects our financial lives regardless of our financial skills or lack thereof.

In John 10:10 (NLT) Jesus said, *"The thief's purpose is to steal and kill and destroy. My purpose is to give them a rich and satisfying life."* We know the thief that Jesus was referring to was the devil. We can ascertain from this statement that the devil, or the enemy, has the ability to influence our livelihood in that he can use various methods to steal and take from us. This can apply to all aspects of our lives whether emotionally, physically, financially, or in some other area.

The good news is Jesus followed up with the statement that He has come to offer us a rich and satisfying life. But the point to understand is how the spirit realm, whether it be of God or the enemy, influences our lives particularly regarding our subject at hand, which is our financial lives.

It's easy to get so caught up in everything we can see in the natural. Not only can we become caught up in all the financial challenges we face in the natural, but we often get caught up in only seeking out natural answers and solutions. While the natural realm is real and viable, we simply cannot forget the unseen spirit realm influencing it.

Remember, it's not flesh and blood or the natural realm that we are fighting (see Ephesians 6:12). It is the dark powers in the spirit realm that are influencing the battles we face financially. While good financial responsibility is important, we can't bear that as the only burden in fixing our money issues. We need to consider the influence of demonic powers and strongholds.

Over the years I have known so many people who feel beat up and condemned because they cannot seem to get ahead financially. Again, I want to be sure to clarify that I am not dismissing the important factors of financial prudence and investing in God's Kingdom through tithes and offerings. Those things must come into order first and foremost. However, in the process of bettering how we are managing these areas, success never comes without failures and mistakes along the way.  Understanding the work of evil spirits when it comes to our money is a key factor in helping overcome the setbacks we experience in the natural realm.

Remember, demons operate harshly.  They attack both when you are at your highest and feeling your best, and they also attack when you are down.  They will look for every chance they can.  They attack in two key ways, one being through financial challenges such as a job or income loss or an unexpected bill; the other way they attack is to get you discouraged and condemned.

Let's talk first about how demons try to defeat you financially through challenges and setbacks.  Remember, according to Ephesians 6:12, we are at war with the demons of darkness, which in turn means they are at war with us.  They war against us using negative circumstances to put us in places of loss, debt, and lack.

It's important to always be cognizant of the fact that demonic power is often at the bottom of many of the challenges we face.  Don't underestimate them or dismiss their involvement. Now, we are not to be fearful of demons because we have authority over them in the Name of Jesus (see Luke 10:19, Mark 16:17).  At the same time, we are to be aware of their works that try to interfere in our daily lives.  1 Peter 5:8-9 says that the devil walks about looking to devour, but that we have the ability to resist his operations through faith.

What we must do is realize that when challenges arise regarding our money quite often demons are involved because they are agents of poverty and lack.  Additionally, some of the repetitive and ongoing work of these evil spirits has been passed down through our bloodline and generations because no one has challenged them.

So how can we know if evil spirits are the key source of our financial issues?  Well first of all, we know because they are authors of all that surrounds human suffering.  But at the same time, there are certain clues as to when you can recognize that a demon, particularly one that has been passed down through generations, is specifically at work.

> 1) When there are repetitive curses, such as certain illnesses, bad habits, or financial issues that were obvious in our parents or grandparents, it's likely that we will carry on the same curses.  Usually there is a demonic stronghold that needs to be addressed. We often dismiss these repetitive occurrences to coincidence or bad habits that we "learned" from parents, when in reality demons are the driving force behind it.  If you came from a poor family, the likelihood of your struggling financially is much higher.  In part it is because we learn by our parent's behavior, but also because demonic entities are working a curse of poverty in the family line.  These evil spirits will continue passing it along unless it's challenged and cast out.

2) You can often know a demon is at work when it seems you can't ever get ahead or experience relief or breakthrough.  It seems like you live from one trial to the next without relief.  In the financial arena it might be an expensive repair bill, followed by an unexpected medical expense, only to be topped off by pay cuts at work.  It comes as one thing after the next.  This is the time to suspect that a stronghold needs to be broken.

3) Whenever you feel like giving up or ignoring a problem completely because it seems there isn't any hope, suspect the work of the enemy.  Sometimes in these cases people end up spending money they don't already have in order to escape thinking of their financial problems.  Demonic spirits want you to feel hopeless or get you to ignore an issue until it grows and gets much worse.  They want to stomp out your determination and resolve and get you emotionally tired until you are either too tired to try or until you do something unwise.  Many times when that happens we think that it's just us feeling tired, when it's really a demon at work.

This last point brings us to the other issue about demonic spirits.  We talked about how they evoke challenges and tragic circumstances, but let's expose for a moment how they also try to make us feel discouraged and condemned.

God is a loving heavenly father and He knows our weaknesses and failures.  Psalm 103:13-14 says, *"Like as a father pitieth his children, so the Lord pitieth them that fear him.  For he knoweth our frame; he remembereth that we are dust."*  God understands your failures and isn't in heaven condemning you for every financial mistake you have made, for every time you overspent at the grocery store, or bought something that deviated you from your "get out of debt" plan.

The devil on the other hand wants to beat you up with your own faults, even the smallest of them.  Now we have to pause and clarify that this is never an excuse to allow poor choices and bad behavior to go unchecked, but I think we understand the balance here.  The point is that the devil works overtime to beat people up with themselves.

There are good Christians who love God that unbeknownst to their fellow pew members feel beat up by their own mistakes so much that they can only see themselves in that light.  Feeling discouraged or condemned about your finances is a tool of the enemy to keep you thinking that the current situation you are in is truly what you deserve.  Some are even convinced that God is so disappointed in them that they cease to pray about their money.

These scenarios are all strongholds that must be broken in the power of Jesus' Name!   In addition to working on your natural financial skills, here are some steps to break the power of financial strongholds:

> 1) In every financial challenge, command the work of the enemy to cease.  Remind Satan that what belongs to you is off limits to him and that every spirit of poverty, debt, and lack is bound!

2) Always pray and call out to God in faith no matter how you feel. You might feel down and like a failure, but pray anyhow. Call upon God to help you. There are scores of Scriptures that remind us that when we call on God, even amidst our failures, He will answer and not turn away.

3) Address any obvious generational issues. Financial problems that were obvious in your parents or grandparents need to be addressed. Not only make the decision to not repeat them, but recognize them enough to speak to them and cast them out in Jesus' authority and declare that they will not be passed down to your children or grandchildren.

4) Break the power of evil spirits through giving. Giving brings you to a realm above the demonic. Jesus explained this when He said lay up treasures in heaven where the earthly curse (which is driven by demons) can't destroy your blessings (see Matthew 6:19-20).

The important thing is to recognize that demon powers very often try to deplete our financial stability and we have to take authority over them or we will struggle to experience money miracles because we are allowing demons to interfere unchallenged. Remember that God has given you the authority over evil spirits. If you don't cast them out, they can continue to influence your finances. Bind them up today so you can be free to enjoy the money miracles God wants for you.

# CHAPTER FIVE
## Releasing Angels of Provision

Angels are key enforcers of God's blessings in our lives. They are servants who come to help us and bring God's resources. They truly are carriers of money miracles!

Think of how many times in scripture angels brought objects of blessings to earth. They were the ones who ascended and descended on Jacob's ladder as vessels who made a connective passageway between heaven and earth. In the days of Jesus, angels we're the reapers who harvested the souls of the earth (see Matthew 13:39). In Revelation 8:3, an angel brought the prayers of the saints upon the altar before God's throne. It was an angel that brought strengthening bread to save Elijah (see 1 Kings 19:5). An angel also came to strengthen Jesus during prayer in The Garden of Gethsemane (see Luke 22:43). We also see that an angel delivered God's calling upon Gideon to deliver Israel from the Midianites (see Judges 6:11-21).
Of course there are countless more examples in the Bible of angels bringing messages or objects of blessings to us from

heaven.  Angels are involved in all aspects of our lives and are working around us, even when we don't realize it.  Therefore, it only stands to reason that they are sent by God to help us, and part of that help includes many aspects of provision including our finances.

One of the most familiar verses in Scripture about angels is Psalm 91:11-12 (NLT) which says, *"For he will order his angels to protect you wherever you go.  They will hold you up with their hands so you won't even hurt your foot on a stone."*

This means that angels are ensuring that life's challenges will not cause you to be tripped up in such a way that you cannot recover or cause you to suffer serious injury.  Angels are watching over you to make certain that you will reach the ultimate destination God has intended for you.  God has already intended that you experience financial peace and stability, so it is obvious angels are involved in this important aspect of your journey.

We also know that angels hearken to the Word of God (see Psalm 103:20).  So when you speak the Word of God in various forms of prayer and prophetic declaration regarding your money, angels are responsive to that and get to work bringing those blessings.

Knowing that angels are both involved in bringing things from heaven to us and that they respond to hearing God's Word declared, then without question they are involved in sending provisions, from heaven regarding your money, that are directly connected to your prayers.

Because of your prayers, angels can bring messages from God to help your financial situation. Remember, it was Daniel's prayers in Daniel 10:13 that brought angelic activity to come against the demonic powers over Persia. Much like the prophets of old, this angelic activity can manifest in the form of a dream, a supernatural vision, or through a simple moment of personal inspiration or revelation. Angels can also manifest in human form, as we see in Hebrews 13:2 which says, *"Be not forgetful to entertain strangers: for thereby some have entertained angels unawares."*

Angels can be involved when an idea suddenly comes to you that you hadn't thought of before. It might be a dream that opened your eyes to see strategies that you hadn't previously considered. Very often during times of divine dreams, as it was with Jacob at Bethel (see Genesis 28:10-17), angels are present in the room.

What's important to know is that angels are at work in God's overall plan for your finances to experience increase and stability. That's why it's important to see every positive encounter regarding your money as something divine. Therefore, when these moments of inspiration come along, rather than dismissing them by thinking "that was just me" or by assuming that it was an insignificant coincidence, instead respond to the thought, dream, or encounter with faith and prayer, seeing it as God is trying to communicate and very likely causing you to be the recipient of a money miracle.

Of course, as people most often do when it comes to demons, they will downplay the activity of angels. They believe that if we are quick to assume that heavenly beings are working continually around us, and if we draw attention to that, we are becoming spooky. I agree some people see demons in every room or object, while others see angels the same way. However, I would rather wrongly assume angels are moving about my house than to dismiss one because it seems excessive to think that way. And, the truth is, you as a child of God aren't likely ever wrong to assume an angel is at work in your midst!

In times of ministry to various congregations, I have literally seen revelatory visions of angels moving about the people with provisions from heaven clenched in their fists, or pouring out provisions through doors or windows of the church or auditorium. In each occasion I felt impressed by the Lord to encourage the people to see themselves receiving those provisions by faith. In some cases I felt the Lord tell me to say that whatever their need was, if they would declare it to be theirs, then that is what the angel would release to them in that room.

What is important to remember is that angels are servants that are sent to minister to us (see Hebrews 1:14). That means they will be involved in financial provision and will come to us on varying occasions to bring increase and resources into our hands.

That said, I am not saying money will appear from nowhere. Yes, we did see a coin appear in a fish's mouth in Jesus' day, so that isn't to say it can't happen or will never happen. I truly believe the multiplication of the loaves and fish in Jesus' ministry was a money miracle. Supply for a multitude literally came from nowhere! But that also isn't how Jesus operated every single day, nor was it the only or most common way God manifested miracles. I believe when the early church laid their possessions at the apostle's feet in Acts 4:34-35, that it was a money miracle because the Bible declares that none of God's people lacked at that time. If you can't call that a miracle, I don't know what is because as long as I have been a Christian I have known quite a few lacking Christians!

What we have to know is that angels sent from God to bring provision into our lives will commonly set up divine circumstances that result in a blessing or total miracle. They may be involved in you meeting that person who then in turn was a key to turning your business around. They are likely part of situations when a person you are indebted to feels suddenly inspired to forgive a debt or handle a bill you couldn't pay. They can even be part of a rearranging of your debt load with the bank. Again, angels with God's blessings in their hands come from heaven to bring money miracles.

I want you to think of the money miracle you need in your personal life right now. Perhaps you might consider writing it down as you are reading this. Maybe you have several financial needs that need a miracle in order to be solved. Don't be discouraged about them. God is listening to your prayers today.

What you don't want to do is complain.  Angels don't respond to complaints, they respond to the sound of God's Word, regardless of the source.  They respond to you speaking God's Word in prayer; it's what moves them as God's servants.  You can activate angels this way, but you deactivate them when you complain and revert to words and actions that are fearful.

Take your needs and begin to activate angels of provision through words of confident faith.  Say things like, "Lord I thank You that provision is a promise that belongs to me.  I pray that angels from heaven would be released right now to bring the provision heaven has made available to me."

Think about it, each time you do this the angels that are in your living room, bedroom or kitchen are becoming active!  They are acting upon what you just said.

Then remind yourself that the more you do that, the more active angels will be in operation.  The more you complain or say things like, "I don't know how I am going to pay that bill!" the more angels will become inactive.

Do you want to see the acceleration of your money miracle today?  Get your angels working for you.  Don't dilute their work and activity through a mixture of faith and confidence that is watered down by words of fear and frustration.

See that angels are involved in your financial breakthrough and blessing.  See that they are in the room where you are seated right now, desiring to enact God's plan and promise to bless you.  Put them to work by what you say and by what you pray. Walk past those temptations to get discouraged and say things you shouldn't because mental pressure is bearing down upon you.  Instead, put the angels of provision to work.  They are skilled and ready to bring money miracles from heaven into your life!

# CHAPTER SIX
## Name Your Miracle

So often the reason many believers do not receive financial blessings from God is because they aren't specific about what they are asking.  This is actually true with everything we pray.  In some cases we are too general, thinking that if we get too specific we are pressuring God for things He probably doesn't want us to have anyhow.  So we pray general prayers like, "Lord, bless So-and-So" or "Lord, I am scared and need my debts paid!"  Yet, perhaps we need to hone in on the specific things we want to see.  If we want to experience money miracles, we need to name the specific miracle we need.

James 4:2-3 (NLT) says, *"Yet you don't have what you want because you don't ask God for it. And even when you ask, you don't get it because your motives are all wrong—you want only what will give you pleasure."*

I want to talk here about both being specific in prayer regarding money and also about keeping a right motive.  Many people erroneously think that somehow if you ask God for big things when it comes to finances that your motive is automatically skewed.  While money is one of the major things affecting people's motives, with the love of it being the root of all evil (see 1 Timothy 6:10), that doesn't mean our motive is wrong just because we ask God specifically for money or financial blessings.

Before we fully discuss money and motives, let's talk about being specific in prayer and how that connects to our motives. One of the key reasons why I believe God wants you to be very specific with what you are praying about is because He wants there to be a deep communion in your relationship to Him.  The verse above says we don't receive from God because we simply don't ask for what we truly want.  We generalize over it as if we believe God would never want us to have what's really on our heart, or perhaps because we think we aren't deserving of it.

If you read James 4:2, it talks about how people fall into the trap of scheming to get things they want rather than go to God.  We need to draw attention to the fact that this is a relatively easy trap to fall into.  If you somehow believe that God doesn't want to hear you specifically state the money miracle you want or need, then instead of bringing it before the Lord it's tempting to look for man-made solutions.  We can end up pressuring people and even resort to manipulation if we are not careful. Families and relatives fall into this scenario quite often when it comes to money issues.  Like me, you have most likely heard all the horror stories of family strife over estates, inheritances, and money borrowing that isn't repaid, and so on.

This is what James was addressing in those verses. When we don't get honest and specific with God about the thing we truly need or even desire, we tend to look to other things and then our motives and actions can quickly become displeasing.

Another reason why it is so very important to name the money miracle you need when you come to God is because it creates personal accountability. When you name something very specifically to God and to yourself, it's a first key step in revealing your motive.

For example, if you pray something like, "Lord, I really want a better home," but what's truly in your heart is to have a mansion of some sort, that internal motive is glossed over by your generalized prayer of just wanting a better house. On the other hand, if you pray, "Lord I want a mansion," you might actually pause and check your heart and think, "Wow, is that a selfish prayer? Do, I really need all that?" Motives come to light with specificity.

This isn't to say God is against you having that better than average home, especially if your line of work or investments have given you the salary for such a thing. However, if we're having to believe for some miracle to occur in order for those indulgences to happen while we can't even pay our rent, then somehow our motive is truly out of whack.

You see, naming your miracle before the Lord puts a thumb on the purity of it is a way of communicating your heart to God so He can nudge you with the voice of His Holy Spirit when you get off track. On the other hand, when your request is in line with heaven, the witness of the Spirit inside you will reassure your heart with faith.

Here is another example: perhaps you are trying to get out of debt today and rather than just writing on your prayer list, "I want to be debt-free," name the specific bills you are praying for to be paid off. It's another level of personal accountability that keeps you focused in your faith for that specific miracle to happen.

When you are general in your prayer about just getting out of debt, you tend to deviate from your faith and it also isn't as effective in preventing new unnecessary spending. However, when you have come to God openly asking Him to help you pay down a specific credit card payment, then you are much more thoughtful about frivolous spending because that specific prayer regarding that credit card will be in the forefront of your thoughts. You are quicker to pause and think, "No, I am not buying that new couch or TV today, because God and I have worked too hard on getting this credit card paid off!" You are much quicker to recall all the times you prayed about it and thanked God for helping you get it paid off, so you aren't quick to add debt back on. Naming your miracle this way creates a greater barrier to wrong choices.

At the same time, if you are working on the "credit card" miracle but truly need a new couch in the meantime, make that a new and specific prayer!  Ask the Lord for a new couch!  God wants you to have nice things, but we must make those things specific matters of prayer.

Think for a moment, what farmer doesn't know what kind of harvest he expects to receive when he plants seed.  Your prayer and your financial giving to God are both seeds for miracles.  It would be silly when you pray and give an offering to the Lord not to know what you expect to receive.  Farmers are very specific about this.  In fact, agriculture today is so fine-tuned they calculate the full yield of the harvest before the seed is planted.

Some people believe that being this specific in prayer isn't a right approach because God may have a different idea about what we need and will say no to some of the things we ask for.  It's true, God definitely can withhold things and say no to certain things simply because He may know things that we, in our limited knowledge, may not have considered.  That is something any good parent will do at times for the good of their children.  However, that should never be a reason not to ask for specific miracles or answers to prayer.

I remember years ago, when my husband and I were newly married, we found a house we wanted to buy.  I so wanted that house!  It was a bit of a stretch on our budget, but not unrealistic, so we prayed and asked the Lord to put that house in our hands.  Well, the house sold to someone else and I was utterly disappointed and felt like our miracle didn't come to pass.  However, just a few months later God opened a door for us in the ministry that was a stepping stone to what we are living in today. Had we bought that house we might not have ever walked through that door; and ultimately God gave us a much better house than that one.

So yes, God can shift us in another direction from what we asked for specifically. In our case, God ultimately gave us our miracle regarding a house, it was just temporarily delayed so He could set up some other things we needed first. I am convinced that had we not been specific over the first house, we wouldn't have experienced the miracles we did over our future home. So be specific in your prayers, God will redirect what needs to be redirected.

I want to encourage you to name your specific money miracle today. There may be more than one. Perhaps your finances are in a difficult place and you need several miracles! It's ok, get specific with God. I would suggest you make a list. I think it's best to start with just two or three things. This way you won't fall back into being too general again because your lengthy list is just too much to remember. Take this handful of specific prayer items and lift them up to God. Speak aloud regarding the needs. Follow up by giving an offering. Name that offering and declare that it will yield answers to prayer regarding the specific needs on your paper. Then keep that list daily before your eyes and thank God in faith that your prayers are producing the miracle you have asked for.

Remember, God wants to perform money miracles in our lives. We can't shy away from that. The more you pray and speak with the Lord about your finances, the more He will be involved. He wants to discuss with you the miracle you desire. He already knows it's in your heart anyhow, so it's pointless to pretend to both God and yourself that it's not on your heart. Instead, the Lord wants conversation with you about it. Money is not a taboo subject with God, even though man-made religion has infused that line of thinking into so many people. Money only ruins people when God gets pushed out of the picture. When you keep God involved daily, when you are open and specific with Him, He will keep you on the right track with financial things. He will help you and meet both your needs and desires. He will see to it that you live in financial stability.

So go ahead and name your money miracle today and let the Lord take over regarding your money. When we put certain principles into action, God is ready and more than willing to bring money miracles into our lives!